MLB's Greatest Teams

NEW YORK YANKEES

Big Buddy Books
An Imprint of Abdo Publishing
abdopublishing.com

Katie Lajiness

abdopublishing.com

Published by Abdo Publishing, a division of ABDO, PO Box 398166, Minneapolis, Minnesota 55439.
Copyright © 2019 by Abdo Consulting Group, Inc. International copyrights reserved in all countries. No part
of this book may be reproduced in any form without written permission from the publisher. Big Buddy Books™
is a trademark and logo of Abdo Publishing.

Printed in the United States of America, North Mankato, Minnesota.
052018
092018

Cover Photo: Rich Schultz/Getty Images.
Interior Photos: 33ft/Depositphotos (p. 7); Abbie Parr/Getty Images (p. 27); AP Images (pp. 11, 17, 22, 28);
    Elsa/Getty Images (pp. 5, 21, 23, 24, 25); Harry Harris/AP Images (p. 23); Jeff Zelevansky/Getty Images
    (p. 13); Jim McIsaac/Getty Images (p. 29); Leon Halip/Getty Images (p. 15); Michael Loccisano/Getty
    Images (p. 9); Murray Becker/AP Images (p. 19); PS/AP Images (p. 22).

Coordinating Series Editor: Tamara L. Britton
Graphic Design: Jenny Christensen

Library of Congress Control Number: 2017962673

Publisher's Cataloging-in-Publication Data

Names: Lajiness, Katie, author.
Title: New York Yankees / by Katie Lajiness.
Description: Minneapolis, Minnesota : Abdo Publishing, 2019. | Series: MLB's greatest
    teams | Includes online resources and index.
Identifiers: ISBN 9781532115189 (lib.bdg.) | ISBN 9781532155901 (ebook)
Subjects: LCSH: Major League Baseball (Organization)--Juvenile literature. | Baseball
    teams--United States--History--Juvenile literature. | New York Yankees (Baseball
    team)--Juvenile literature. | Sports teams--Juvenile literature.
Classification: DDC 796.35764--dc23

Contents

Major League Baseball

League Play

There are two leagues in MLB. They are the American League (AL) and the National League (NL). Each league has 15 teams and is split into three divisions. They are east, central, and west.

The New York Yankees is one of 30 Major League Baseball (MLB) teams. The team plays in the American League East **Division**.

Throughout the season, all MLB teams play 162 games. The season begins in April and can continue until November.

In 1929, the Yankees became the first team to make numbers part of the uniform. All teams wore numbers by 1932.

A Winning Team

The Yankees team is from New York City, New York. The team's colors are deep blue, white, and gray.

The team has had good seasons and bad. But time and again, the Yankees players have proven themselves. Let's see what makes the Yankees one of MLB's greatest teams!

Fast Facts

HOME FIELD: Yankee Stadium

TEAM COLORS: Deep blue, white, and gray

TEAM SONG: "New York, New York" by Frank Sinatra

PENNANTS: 40

WORLD SERIES TITLES:
1923, 1927, 1928, 1932, 1936, 1937, 1938, 1939, 1941, 1943, 1947, 1949, 1950, 1951, 1952, 1953, 1956, 1958, 1961, 1962, 1977, 1978, 1996, 1998, 1999, 2000, 2009

CANADA

UNITED STATES OF AMERICA

MEXICO

CANADA

LAKE ONTARIO

New York

Vermont

Massachusetts

Pennsylvania

Connecticut

Bronx

New Jersey

ATLANTIC OCEAN

N
W E
S

Yankee Stadium

The team was first called the Highlanders. It shared a field with the New York Giants until 1922. The original Yankee Stadium opened the next year.

In 1923, the Yankees held their first World Series in the new stadium. The team won its first-ever **championship** in a game against the Giants.

The new Yankee Stadium opened in 2009. It can seat more than 47,000 fans.

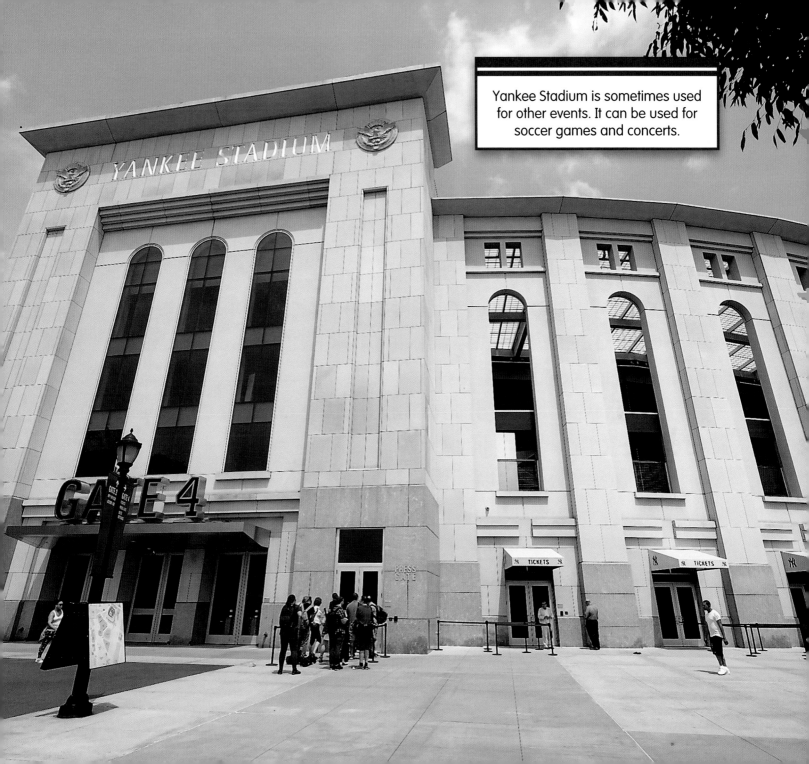

Yankee Stadium is sometimes used for other events. It can be used for soccer games and concerts.

Then and Now

The Yankees team began in 1901 in Baltimore, Maryland. Frank Farrell and Bill Devery bought the team in 1903. The ball club moved to New York soon after. In 1913, the team changed its name to the Yankees.

The Yankees' first 18 seasons were hard. Then, the team won 11 **pennants** and eight World Series during the 1920s and 1930s.

Over the years, the Yankees have had nicknames like the Bronx Bombers and the Pinstripers. Sometimes, the team's rivals call it the Evil Empire.

The Yankees were successful throughout the 1940s. The team won five **pennants** and four World Series. Another winning period lasted from the late 1950s to the early 1960s.

From 1982 to 1994, the Yankees never made it to the **postseason**. Then in 1996, the team's luck changed. From 1996 to 2000, the Yankees won four World Series titles.

Then, after another eight-year World Series losing streak, the team began rebuilding. It won another World Series in 2009. Since then, the team has worked hard to build a strong **roster**.

The 1912 Yankees were the first team to wear pinstripes.

Highlights

The Yankees have won 27 World Series titles and 40 AL **pennants**. The team has played 19 seasons with 100 or more wins. This is more than any other team in MLB.

The Yankees hold spring training at George M. Steinbrenner Field in Tampa, Florida.

The top team from each AL and NL division goes to the playoffs. Each league also sends one wild-card team. One team from the AL and one from the NL will win the pennant. The two pennant winners then go to the World Series!

The Yankees have had much success throughout history. But the most famous is when the team gained Babe Ruth from the Red Sox.

The superstar batter led the Yankees to three AL **championships** in a row. And, he helped earn the team's first World Series title in 1923.

In June 1948, the Yankees celebrated Yankee Stadium's twenty-fifth anniversary. There, the team honored Yankees hero Babe Ruth.

Famous Managers

Joe McCarthy is the most successful manager in the team's history. Under McCarthy, the Yankees earned eight AL **pennants** from 1932 to 1946. And, he led the team to seven World Series titles.

He coached famous players such as Babe Ruth, Lou Gehrig, and Joe DiMaggio. McCarthy was **inducted** into the National Baseball Hall of Fame in 1957.

Over 15 years, McCarthy's team earned almost 96 wins per season.

Joe Torre began managing the team in 1996. He guided the Yankees to 92 wins his first year. By the end of the season, Torre led the team to a World Series win.

Torre managed the Yankees until 2007. During this time, the team won four World Series titles and six AL **pennants**. Torre was **inducted** into the National Baseball Hall of Fame in 2014.

Under Torre's leadership, the Yankees made it to 12 straight playoff seasons.

Star Players

Babe Ruth RIGHT FIELDER, #3

1920 – 1934

Babe Ruth was the top AL player during his first 12 seasons with the Yankees. He led the league in batting 11 times, and in home runs ten times. Most people consider Babe Ruth the greatest baseball player of all time. The National Baseball Hall of Fame was founded in 1936. Babe Ruth was one of the first to be **inducted**.

Joe DiMaggio CENTER FIELDER, #5

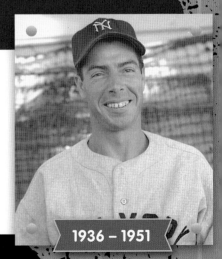

1936 – 1951

Joe DiMaggio is another of the greatest players who ever lived. He played for the Yankees his entire **career**. On the field, he could do it all. His 1941 56-game hitting streak is one that many believe will never be broken. In 1955, DiMaggio was inducted into the National Baseball Hall of Fame.

Mickey Mantle CENTER FIELDER, #7

An iconic baseball player, Mickey Mantle played for the Yankees his entire **career**. From 1951 to 1968, he hit about 36 home runs per season. Mantle earned the AL's **Most Valuable Player (MVP)** Award three times. He was **inducted** into the Baseball Hall of Fame in 1974.

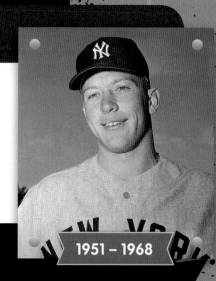

1951 – 1968

Derek Jeter SHORTSTOP, #2

The Yankees **drafted** Derek Jeter in 1992 in the first round. He played with the Yankees his entire career. During his first full MLB season, he helped the Yankees win the 1996 World Series. Then he helped win four more World Series titles. Jeter became team captain in 2003. He **retired** in 2015.

1995 – 2014

23

2008 –

Brett Gardner OUTFIELDER, #11

Brett Gardner helped his team win the 2009 World Series title. In 2013, he led the AL in **triple plays**. Because of his superstar plays, he became a member of the 2015 All-Star team. Later, Gardner's skills won him the 2016 **Gold Glove Award**.

Didi Gregorius SHORTSTOP, #18

Didi Gregorius joined the Yankees in 2015. In his first season, he almost won the AL Gold Glove Award. His first year, he hit a **career**-high of nine home runs. The following season, Gregorius hit 20 homers. Then in June 2017, Gregorius made his fiftieth home run!

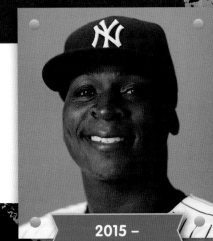

2015 –

Gary Sánchez CATCHER, #24

In August 2016, Gary Sánchez earned AL Player of the Week for two straight weeks. That same month, Sánchez won AL Player of the Month and **Rookie** of the Month. In August 2017, he hit 12 home runs. That is a success made by other greats like Babe Ruth and Joe DiMaggio.

2015 –

Aaron Judge RIGHT FIELDER, #99

2016 –

In his second season, Aaron Judge earned three straight AL Rookie of the Month Awards. Then in June 2017, he was the AL Player of the Month. Three months later, Judge hit his fiftieth home run! That made him the first rookie in MLB history to do so.

25

Final Call

The best players from both leagues come together each year for the All-Star Game. This game does not count toward the regular season records. It is simply to celebrate the best players in MLB.

The Yankees team has a long, rich history. It has played in 40 World Series and it has won 27 titles.

Even during losing seasons, true fans have stuck by the team. Many believe the Yankees will remain one of the greatest teams in MLB.

The Yankees celebrate in a win against the Minnesota Twins in the 2017 AL Wild-Card Game.

Through the Years

1903

The Yankees team became a member of the American League.

1912

Pinstripes were added to the Yankees uniform. This look became the most famous design for sports uniforms.

1927

Babe Ruth broke his own MLB record by hitting his sixtieth home run.

1946

The Yankees played their first night game at Yankee Stadium.

1938

A record 81,841 fans attended a Yankees **doubleheader** against the Boston Red Sox.

28

1956

Don Larsen pitches the only **perfect game** in World Series history. The Yankees win 2-0 over Brooklyn.

1976

The remodeled Yankee Stadium opened. In their first game in the updated stadium, the Yankees beat the Minnesota Twins.

1999

A monument to Joe DiMaggio was shown in Monument Park near Yankee Stadium.

2016

For the twenty-fourth year in a row, the Yankees posted a winning record. This was the second-longest stretch in MLB history. The first-longest stretch was the team's own streak of 39 winning seasons!

Glossary

career a period of time spent in a certain job.

championship a game, a match, or a race held to find a first-place winner.

division a number of teams grouped together in a sport for competitive purposes.

doubleheader two games played one right after the other on the same day.

draft a system for professional sports teams to choose new players.

Gold Glove Award annually given to the MLB players with the best fielding experience.

induct to officially introduce someone as a member.

Most Valuable Player (MVP) the player who contributes the most to his or her team's success.

pennant the prize that is awarded to the champions of the two MLB leagues each year.

perfect game a baseball game in which a pitcher allows no hits, no runs, and no opposing batter to reach first base.

postseason a period of time immediately after the regular season. Teams will play against each other in a series of games to find a winner.

retire to give up one's job.

rookie a player who is new to the major leagues until he meets certain criteria.

roster an orderly list of people belonging to a professional sports group.

triple play a play in baseball by which the team in the field causes three runners to be put out.

Online Resources | **Booklinks** NONFICTION NETWORK FREE! ONLINE NONFICTION RESOURCES

To learn more about the New York Yankees, visit **abdobooklinks.com**. These links are routinely monitored and updated to provide the most current information available.

Index